From Tadpole to Frog

By Kathleen Weidner Zoehfeld

SCHOLASTIC INC.

New York   Toronto   London   Auckland
Sydney   Mexico City   New Delhi   Hong Kong

Photo Credits

All photographs copyright © 2010 Dwight R. Kuhn Photography, Dexter, Maine, except: cover, page 1: Alamy
Images/Ashway; cover inset: Alamy Images/Andrew Darrington; page 3: Alamy Images/O.D. vande Veer.
There are many different species of frogs in the world. The time it takes for a tadpole
to develop into a frog can be different, depending on the species of frog.
The frog shown in this book is the wood frog.

ISBN 978-0-545-27337-4

12 11 10 9 8 7 6 5 4 3 2 1   11 12 13 14 15 16/0

Printed in the U.S.A. 40
This edition first printing, January 2011

In the spring, you may see frog eggs in a pond.

Each egg looks like a ball of clear jelly with a dark center.

A clump of frog eggs is called frog **spawn.**

Inside the eggs, tiny **tadpoles** are growing.

At first, they look like small,
dark specks.

In a few days, a little head
and tail take shape.

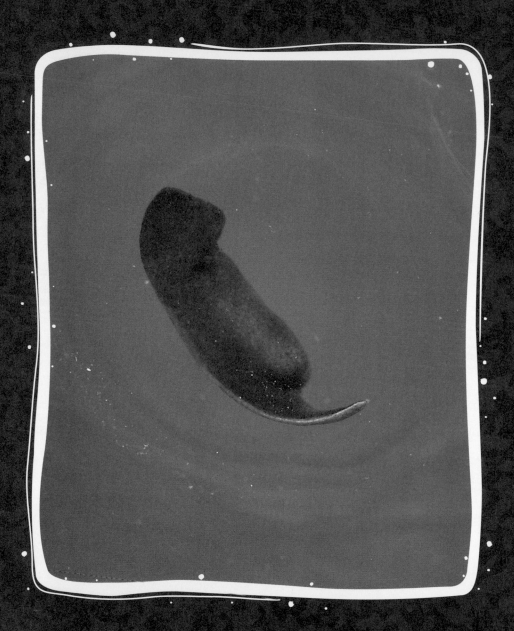

Soon the tadpoles wiggle out
of their eggs.

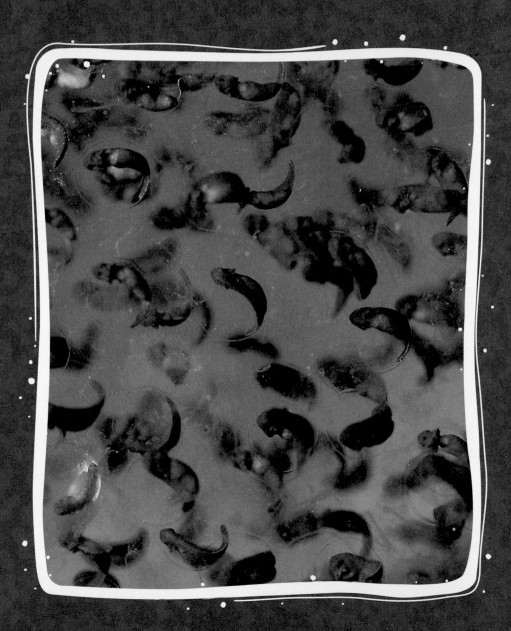

Gills on the outside of a tadpole's body help it breathe underwater.

gills

After eating the jelly of its egg,
the tadpole has grown.

The tadpole's strong tail helps it swim.

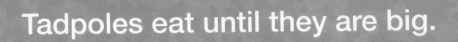
Tadpoles eat until they are big.

They do not look like frogs yet!

Soon the tadpole has grown two **hind legs**. And the tadpole's gills have moved inside its body.

Lungs are beginning to form inside the tadpole's body, too.

Now and then, it puts its head above the water to take a breath.

As the tadpole's lungs grow stronger, its gills shrink away.

Two front legs grow where its gills once were.

Soon the tadpole's mouth has
become wider.

The tadpole starts to eat small bugs when it is hungry.

For a few more weeks, the tadpole's tail shrinks.

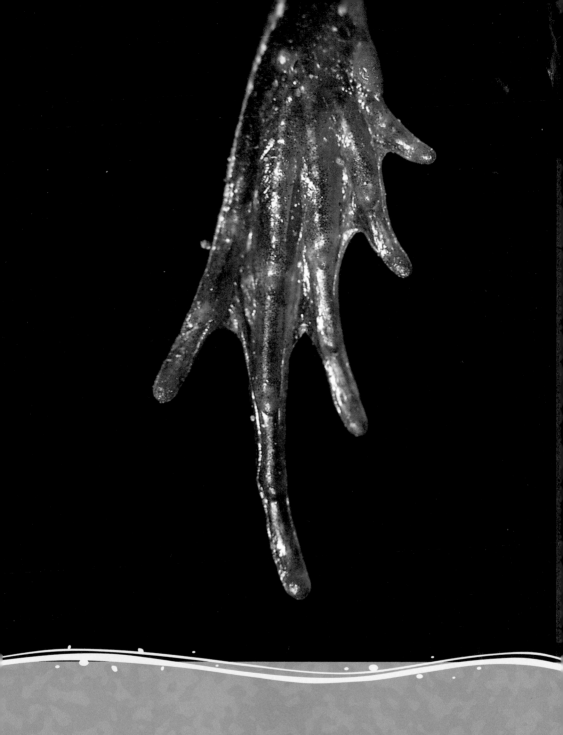

Now the tadpole's strong legs and **webbed feet** help it swim.

The tadpole has changed into a small frog! The frog spends some of its time on land and some in the water.

The little frog catches bugs and worms in its wide mouth.

After a few years, the frog is fully grown.

Every spring, there will be
new frog eggs in the pond.

Glossary

Gills—a part of the body most water animals use for breathing

Hind legs—the rear or back legs of an animal

Lungs—parts of an animal's body used for breathing

Spawn—any type of egg that is laid in water

Tadpoles—very young frogs or toads

Webbed feet—any type of feet with thin, flat folds of skin connecting the toes